Options Trading For Beginners:

How To Start

Table of Contents

Introduction
Chapter 1: All About Options Trading
Chapter 2: Create a Trading Plan
Chapter 3: Analyzing Potential Trades
Chapter 4: Strategies to Try
Chapter 5: Mistakes to Avoid
Conclusion
Description

© Copyright 2018 by _____ All rights reserved.

The follow eBook is reproduced below with the goal of providing information that is as accurate and reliable as possible. Regardless, purchasing this eBook can be seen as consent to the fact that both the publisher and the author of this book are in no way experts on the topics discussed within and that any recommendations or suggestions that are made herein are for entertainment purposes only. Professionals should be consulted as needed prior to undertaking any of the actions endorsed herein.

This declaration is deemed fair and valid by both the American Bar Association and the Committee of Publishers Association and is legally binding throughout the United States.

Furthermore, the transmission, duplication or reproduction of any of the following work including specific information will be considered an illegal act irrespective of whether it is done electronically or in print. This extends to creating a secondary or tertiary copy of the work or a recorded copy and is only allowed with express written consent from the Publisher. All additional rights reserved.

The information in the following pages is broadly considered to be a truthful and accurate account of facts and as such any inattention, use or misuse of the information in question by the reader will render any resulting actions solely under their purview. There are no scenarios in which the publisher or the original author of this work can be in any fashion deemed liable for any hardship or damages that may befall them after undertaking information described herein.

Additionally, the information in the following pages is intended only for informational purposes and should thus be thought of as universal. As befitting its nature, it is presented without assurance regarding its prolonged validity or interim quality. Trademarks that are mentioned are done without written consent and can in no way be considered an endorsement from the trademark holder.

Introduction

Congratulations on downloading *Option Trading For Beginners: How To Start*

and thank you for doing so. While the steep barrier to entry surrounding the stock market means that it is out of reach for many people, options trading offers an affordable alternative that still promises the opportunity for plenty of profit.

Getting started can still be somewhat complicated, however, which is why the following chapters will discuss everything you need to know to dip your toe in options trading without ending up all wet. First, you will learn about what sets options trading apart from securities trading. Next, you will learn to create a trading plan that will prevent you from losing your shirt.

From there you will learn about the technical indicators to watch when it comes to picking potential trades as well as plenty of starter strategies to try. Finally, you will find an assortment of common mistakes that new options traders make as well as steps you can take to ensure you do not follow in their footsteps.

There are plenty of books on this subject on the market, thanks again for choosing this one! Every effort was made to ensure it is full of as much useful information as possible, please enjoy!

Chapter 1: All About Options Trading

One of many types of securities, including bonds or stocks, options are a type of contract that gives their owner the opportunity, not the obligation to either sell or buy a specific asset for a specific price during a specific window of time. Additionally, it can be considered a type of contract that is binding is regards to a narrow group of properties and terms.

While the ideas behind them may seem opaque, they are actually used quite commonly in everyday situations. The basics behind options are frequently called into play when it comes to buying a house if the seller and the buyer negotiate an agreement that says the buyer will have the option to purchase the property at a set price in 2 months once they have raised sufficient capital. There is usually a fee associated with this, but then the buyer and seller are locked into the agreement no matter how the market changes in that period of time. This can be extremely good for the buy if the market fluctuates substantially in that time while also not costing them any risk as they have the option to not purchase if the deal would ultimately not work out in their favor.

It is important to understand that an option is simply a contract that relates to an associated asset which makes it a type of derivative which is any type of security that doesn't have innate value on its own. This includes things like indexes or stocks but not commodities. When employees are offered the opportunity to by company stock at a fixed point, that is another type of option. All told, every type of option can be divided into two categories those that are puts and those that are calls.

Calls allow their owners to buy a specific type of asset for a certain price and are most closely akin to taking a position that could be considered long on a certain stock. Those who purchase calls are specifically hoping that their related stocks with increase drastically by the time the option is ready to end.

. If you place a call order you are implying that you feel as though the underlying security that the option is related to is going to increase in value before the point the option expires and if you place a put you are saying that you believe the price is going to drop before the option expires.

Options are also classified as either European or American though the names have nothing to do with the location of origin. Rather, the rules or the two classes of options are different because American options can be exercised at any point prior to the time they expire and European options can only be exercised at the point and time they expire which makes them riskier, especially for new investors who can easily miscalculate market movement.

Furthermore, European and American options are both what is known as vanilla options which means they are always going to behave in the ways outlined above. There are also exotic options which can various based on several types of criteria that may or may not be explicitly stated at the type of purchase. As long as you feel as though you are a novice investor, you should not worry about exotic options. Finally, regardless of the type of option it is, it can be either long or short. A short option is one that expires in 24 hours or less while long options will expire in either years or at least months. As an investor, you are going to likely be looking into long options if you hope to see the best returns.

Finally, all options, be they puts or calls, can be said to be either short or long. Short options have an expiration date of either minutes, days or hours and long options are those that do not expire for either months or years. Short options are better for daily trading as it does not take much movement to be successful, while long options are better when used as a type of investment strategy and can also be called LEAPS or long equity anticipation security.

Along with the options they trade, options traders can be classified as either holders, who buy options, or writers, who sell options. Additionally, holders and writers tend to focus on either calls or puts to specialize in. As a general rule, holders are always in a stronger position of power because if they choose to act on an option, the writer who is selling the option has to agree to sell, even if it isn't in their best interests to do so at that particular moment. Likewise, if holders see a plan not coming together, they can simply walk away, virtually ensuring that they minimize their losses, if nothing else.

Options lingo

If you ultimately plan on investing in the options market successfully, it is important that you have a clear idea of what many of the common phrases you are going to see and hear bandied about actually mean. Keep the following terms in mind and you will sound like a proper investor in no time flat.

Strike Price : The price of the underlying stock at the moment you purchase either a call or a put is referred to as the strike price.

Exercise : When the terms of your option become favorable enough that you are interested in acting on it then you exercise the option to purchase or sell the underlying stock related to the option.

Trading out : If you are the writer on an option and the holder exercises it at a price that you feel it could do better than, then you can buy it back from them and recreate the option in hopes of getting a better deal. This is what is referred to as trading out and it is the outcome for a vast majority of all options trades. Somewhere around 10 percent of all trades are exercised completely, 50 percent are traded out and the remainer expire uselessly.

Listed: If an option is listed on a national exchange it is said to be listed. Listed options have clear strike prices as well as clear expiration dates which makes them a great place for new options traders to start. Listed options are most likely going to deal in 100 shares of stock of the related stock.

Underlying stock: The underlying stock of an option is the specific stock that the option is dealing in.

In the money: On a call, if the price of the underlying stock rises above the stock price then that option is said to be in the money.

Intrinsic value: When a call is in the money, the difference between the current price and the strike price is referred to as its intrinsic value.

Volatility: If the underlying stock related to a particular option is prone to extreme fluctuations in price with little warning then it is said to have a high level of volatility.

Premium: The total price of the option in question including a combination of stock price, strike price, time value, and volatility.

Understanding influences

Price of the underlying asset: While they often will not move at the same speed or for the same amounts, an option is always going to follow the lead of its underlying asset. As such, you can always expect the price of related calls to increase along with rising asset prices; while puts will always decrease and vice versa.

Intrinsic value: The amount of value that an option is going to hold onto, even at the very end of its lifespan, is known as the intrinsic value. When working with a call option you can find the intrinsic value by taking the current price of the underlying asset and dividing that by the difference between the strike price and the current price. When it comes to finding the intrinsic value of a put option, the process is mostly the same; to start, you subtract the amount the underlying asset is currently worth from its strike price before dividing that number by the current stock price.

Time value: The amount of time that an option has until it expires is directly related to how likely that same option is going to ultimately end in a profit greater than the intrinsic value before things are said and done. To determine the amount of time value that the option you are considering currently offers you will want to find the current price of the option and subtract from it the amount of intrinsic value that the same option currently has. It is common for options to hold onto 70 percent of their total value, or more, during the first half of their lifetime before losing value much more rapidly after that point. It is also important to note that time value can change dramatically based on the volatility of the underlying asset both in the moment and based on its expectations in the future. As a general rule, the lower the time value, the more stable the option is likely to be.

Primary uses for options investing

Professional options investors utilize options in two main ways, to minimize the risk of other investments or to bet on the way the market is going to be heading in the near future. Betting on the market is referred to as speculation and options traders who can read the market can use it to make money regardless of the direction the market is heading in. Speculators need to know how the market is going to move but also the speed at which it is going to do so which is why speculation can be responsible for huge financial swings in both directions. The volatility comes from the fact that each option is 100 shares so relatively small movements in the underlying stock can lead to significant movement in related options.

While speculation can be risky, using options to hedge other investments is anything but.

Chapter 2: Create a Trading Plan

If you are interested in ensuring that you do more than simply avoid losing your shirt when you start options trading on the regular, then the first thing you are going to need to do is create the type of personalized trading plan that ensures it is more likely to make a profit than not when used in the wild. It isn't enough just to create the plan; however, you are also going to need to have the dedication and mental determination to stick with it, even when your emotions are in overdrive, which is a skill that can only reliably be counted on with practice.

Consider your strengths and weaknesses: In order to ensure that the plan that you end up with is one that you will actually be able to make use of, the first thing you are going to need to do is to consider your level of experience with the market you favor in the past and how successful you have been at trading previously. The fast paced nature of day trading means that it is going to take more innate knowledge and skill than some of the other investment markets that you could start off in. As such, it is important that when it comes to creating a plan that works for you, you also consider various other weaknesses that may hinder you when it comes to day trading and also those skills that will be able to give you an edge over the competition.

During this personal evaluation, you are going to want to be certain that you take a look at yourself through an analytical lens as overestimating your abilities will do nothing except set you up for bigger losses, sooner than later. This analysis isn't a test, there are no winners or losers, the goal is to get as accurate view of the whole picture as possible, nothing more.

Be aware of the obstacles in your path: While you will likely have a few personal issues that may need to be worked through in order to achieve trading success, it is important to also consider any other obstacles that might be standing in your way so that you can approach them properly. These obstacles can be anything from the limited amount of time that you are ultimately going to have to work with to simply not having the level of capital you would prefer in order to get started in the most effective way possible.

It doesn't matter what the barrier is, it only matters how you are going to circumvent it. Having a clear idea of what may get in the way of your future success will allow you to prepare for it ahead of time and mitigate its long-term impact as much as possible. Taking the time to work through this step properly will help improve not only your overall success rate but your bankable profits as well.

Find your proper level of risk: In order to determine the proper amount of risk for you, the first thing you will need to keep in mind is how much capital you are going to be working with to start, as well as what that money means to you personally. If you were able to put together a few grand relatively easy to try something new, then your total risk is going to be low. However, if it took you months of hard work to come up with the same amount, then your relative risk is going to be higher, though the amount in question didn't change. This will allow you to determine the amount you can put into each trade, so you never trade more than you can afford to lose.

The right amount of risk for you is going to be different than that of anyone else which is why it is important to avoid pre-generated plans and instead take the time to craft your own unique plan instead. If you are risk-averse then you are going to want to make fewer trades overall, and only move forward when the trade you have identified has a fairly substantial chance of success. On the other hand, if you aren't afraid of a little risk then you will need to make more trades overall to balance out your overall trade percentage as a greater percentage of your trades are going to be unsuccessful.

Regardless, a good rule of thumb is that you will only want to move forward on trades that have a chance of paying out a minimum of 300 times what your initial investment is going to be. The amount you invest compared to the amount you stand to gain is what is known as a risk-reward ratio and it can be found by taking the amount of the return and dividing it by the amount you are putting down on the trade in the first place. This number should always be greater than 3 if you want them to be worth your while in the long run. It is important to keep in mind that this number will only show how profitable a given trade is likely to be, not how likely it is that it will work out in your favor.

Choose the right moment : After you have a general idea of what your investment levels are going to be, you will then want to consider how these numbers translate into successful trades which means finding the right entry and exit points to support your new plan. This is very important, especially with short-term trades as it can be very easy to overshoot your mark and turn a winning trade into a losing one in the process. While staying in as long as possible to ride a winning trade might make sense in theory, in reality, it is just going to end up costing you more in lost profits in the long run.

When it comes to choosing the right exit points you will always want to focus on the limits for your tolerance for risk and avoid changing the exit point once the trade has started, no matter what. On the other hand, when it comes to choosing profitable entry points you will never want to make a move on a trade that doesn't mesh with your own natural tolerance for risk. It doesn't matter how good of a deal a trade might be if it falls outside the level of risk that you are comfortable with then you will never be able to act on it as effectively as possible.

Once you know the types of trades you are looking for in general then you will be able to look into various types of day trading strategies that support those types of trades. There are countless different strategies available, as long as your plan is profitable then you should easily be able to find one that fits your plan like a glove.

Asses your plan: Once you have a plan in place, the next thing you are going to want to do is to try it out for approximately one month in order to determine if it is effective or not. If it is, then great, otherwise you will need to rework it until it is successful approximately 60 percent of the time. While that might sound low, the fact of the matter is that no trading plan is going to be 100 percent reliable and a plan that is 60 percent reliable is going to be enough to turn a profit in the long run. Once you have given your plan some time to work, it is important to stick with it, assuming it is successful in the general sense, even when you have a streak of bad luck. Changing your plan too often is only going to lead to confusing results that will make it difficult for you to determine if you are on the right track. Stick with a single plan and you are likely to see much better results overall.

Dedicate yourself to your plan: Once you have a plan in place, especially one that is profitable more than 50 percent of the time, it is important to stick to it with an almost machine like determination. The only way that you can reliably rely on the results that you have gathered is if you stick with your plan no matter what, even if you are having a run of bad luck and feel as though being bound by rules is only holding you back. The fact of the matter is that if you followed the signs that your plan indicated would be successful and then something happened that was outside of your control you should be proud of yourself for sticking to the plan as opposed to angry things did not work out. That level of dedication is hard to reach and in the long run, will be worth more than one individual trade payout. Remember, trading successfully in the long term means listing to the numbers to the exclusion of all else.

Chapter 3: Analyzing Potential Trades

Technical indicators come into play in options trading when you need to determine turning points for underlying stock and the trends that get them to this point. When used correctly, they can help to determine the optimal time to buy or sell and also predict movement cycles. In general, technical indicators are calculated based on the pricing pattern of the underlying stock. Relevant data includes highs and lows, opening price, volume and closing price. They typically take into account the data regarding a stock's price from the past few periods, based on the charts the person who is doing the analyzing prefers.

This information is then used to identify trends that show what has been happening regarding a specific stock and then using past information to determine likely results for the future. Positive trends are known as uptrends and negative trends are known as reversals, but these aren't the only types of trends you are likely to come across. Horizontal trends are those that are purely middle of the road and indicate that the market is currently moving much at all and are an even mixture of highs and lows that ultimately don't amount to much of anything.

Trends can vary radically in size and a general rule of thumb is that the longer a given trend is, the stronger it is as well. If you find a trend in your preferred timeframe that seems to cut off suddenly, the first thing you should do is to ensure that what you are looking at isn't simply part of a trend that takes place over a longer timeframe. The easiest way to ensure you are accurately determining your trends is to consult charts that cover both the short and the long-term.

Technical indicators come in both leading and lagging varieties. Indicators that lag are based on data that already exists and make it easier to determine if a trend is in the process of forming or if the stock in question is simply trading within a range. The stronger the trend that the lagging indicator pinpoints the greater the chance it is going to continue into the future. They typically drop the ball when it comes to predicting potential pullbacks or rally points, however.

When it comes to leading indicators, they are mainly useful when you are looking to predict the point in the future where the price of a specific stock is going to crash or rally. More often than not, these are going to be momentum indicators which, as the name implies, gauge the strength of the movement the underlying stock is going to undertake. Leading indicators tend to come in handy when you need to determine if the price the stock in question has reached is untenable in the long run and, if so, when the slowdown of the current trend is likely to occur. Due to the fact that both oversold and overbought stocks are guaranteed to experience a pullback, knowing when this move is going to occur will come in handy more likely than not.

Both of these indicators can be useful, as long as you understand what it is that you are looking for. They are also frequently used in conjunction with one another as you will often find yourself in need of both the types of trends that are starting to form as well as how long they are going to last if you want things to work out as effectively as possible. Generally speaking, you will want to stick to at least three different indicators.

Map it: Once you have found the trend you think you are looking for; the next step is going to be creating a trendline as a way of qualifying what it is that you have found. To do this all you need to do is place a straight line through the data points you are curious about, specifically the high points for a negative trend and the low points for a positive trend. What you will have created is then known as a resistance line and it is a physical representation of the market's ability to push back on the asset in question whenever it gets either too high or too low. While not always useful when it comes to predicting what the asset in question is going to do next, it will tell you the overall limits of how the asset is likely to move.

Once you are finished drawing the primary line, the next thing you will need to do is to draw a line on either side of the primary trend line to show ancillary levels of resistance and support. This channel will then either move positively, negatively or horizontally. If you extend this channel to a long enough point, then you should be able to determine where the price is likely to split from the norm which indicates the period when you will likely need to act if you want to generate the maximum profit possible.

Useful indicators

MACD Moving average convergence divergence: When it comes to confirming a trend that you have noticed, MACD is the choice of professional traders everywhere. When utilized properly it measures the difference of two averages that have already been smoothed out to minimize random noise. If this average ends up being greater than the moving average, then the trend is positive while if it is less the trend is negative. The value of the MACD indicator will be 0 at the point where the averages intersect. The direction at which they cross should correlate to the trend that you uncover.

To utilize MACD properly you need to first determine a longer and a shorter moving average. With this done, MACD works by taking into account the value left over by subtracting the longer from the shorter before then plotting the results out over between 12 and 26 days. If the two averages line up with the shorter above the longer then you know that momentum is increasing while the opposite is also true. This situation shows that you should hold off on any trades as the situation is likely going to improve sooner than later.

When plotting out the MACD you will also want to plot a moving average at the same time as this will help you understand when the momentum is likely to shift. Plotting the moving average of the MACD is known as the signal line and it is an option in most trading platforms. When the MACD line crosses at a point above the signal line then the trend is bullish and if it crosses below then it is bearish. If the results are bullish then this is a strong indicator that the trend is soon going to reverse.

While this tool can be useful if you are curious about the short-term direction the underlying assets you favor are going to move, it has its limitations as well. Specifically, it can generate mixed signals if the market is in a state of high volatility as numerous small movements tend to generate false signals.

Additionally, as a lagging indicator, it can generate numerous different signals if the period of time you are tracking is exceedingly long. Finally, it is important to keep in mind that it is largely useless when it comes to comparing a pair of assets that are sitting at different price points. Remember, it is useful for comparing a pair of moving averages, not for comparing assets directly.

RSI: The relative strength index (RSI) is typically used to calculate results in increments of three days and measures the total sum of positive days and negative days before calculating a value with a range between 0 and 100. If the movement of the underlying asset in this period is generally positive, then the indicator will end up closer to 100 and if the movement is negative the result will be closer to 0. As such, if the result is close to 50 then the results are considered to be neutral.

RSIs are especially useful when it comes to monitoring oscillators which are technical indicators which vary between a pair of values that can be considered extreme with the goal of determining the current conditions of the asset in questions in terms of whether or not it is currently oversold or overbought. The closer to the high end value the oscillator goes, the more likely the related asset is to reach an overbought status, while the same goes for a low end value and the oversold status. The RSI then comes in as a way of telling you if the related asset movement you are seeing is due to one of these variables or if there is still room there to make a profit.

To determine the RSI, you use the following formula: 100/1+RS where RSI=100- and RS is equal to the average of the close on the days that saw an overall positive asset movement divided by the average of the close on the days that saw an overall negative asset movement. Typically, the indicator of a position that is overbought is 70 or higher, while the indicator of a position that is oversold is 30 or below. These can be reset to 80 and 20 respectively if you tend to have a higher tolerance for trading risk.

If you prefer to enter after a pullback to the current price has occurred, then you may find that you are more interested in the 50-day average as you will want to take a long position if it rises above the 200-day average while at the same time the RSI is dropping. On the other hand, if you find yourself in a situation where the 50-day average drops below the 200-day average, while at the same time the RSI is rising, then you will want to take a short position related to the underlying assets in question.

When it comes to ensuring you are using the RSI as effectively as possible, many traders find that it is best to compare the results they find to those found through the use of the moving average crossovers that can be applied in the short-term. This goes for both the moving average in the 2-day and the 10-day timeframe as both can provide you with the points of crossover you are looking for to determine the likelihood that the price is going to reverse in the near future. These crossovers are likely to coincide with either the 70/30 or 80/20 spit that you established with your RSI. It can also easily be used in conjunction with any momentum-based indicators you are using in order to provide a superior means of determining both entry and exit points.

The 3-day RSI is also worth considering in addition to the standard RSI as it will often show you how to maximize your profit while at the same time ensuring your risk remains at an acceptable level, whatever that ends up meaning to you. If you are holding a long position, then once the RSI moves above 70 you can assume that the best option is to take half of your profits, choose a new exit point, and split the difference when it comes to riding out the trend and playing it safe. If you are taking a short position, then you will want to look for an RSI that is lower than 30.

Average directional index: The average directional index can be thought of as a sort of guidepost that confirms the signals that other technical indicators uncover. Once a trend has been identified successfully, the average directional index can then more easily determine its strength when compared to the other trends that are currently taking place. The average directional index features a combination of directional indicators that are negative and positive, so they can track trends regardless of their direction. They are then unified in a way that determines the overall strength of the trend.

As an oscillating indicator, the average directional index ranges between 100 and 0. The low end indicates that the trend is essentially flat and without volatility while the high end indicates that the stock is virtually moving straight up and down very quickly. This indicator is only useful when it comes to measuring the overall strength of the trend, not which direction it is moving in or is likely to move in any time soon.

When it comes to keeping an eye out for these types of signals, if a trend moves from above the 40 mark to below it, then you can safely assume that the current trend you are following is slowing which means it is likely time to alter your trading strategy or to close out any positions you may still be holding on to. Nevertheless, if you see a trend start below 20 and then increase to near 40 or above then you can assume that a neutral market is beginning to pick up steam and a major trend is likely forming.

This is why it is so important to keep in mind the point where the positive and negative directional indexes cross. If the negative direction index crosses the positive moving upward, then you can assume the market is bullish, otherwise, you can assume the market is bearish.

Chapter 4: Strategies to Try

While the early days of your options trading career are likely to consist of a persistent feeling of information overload, there are certain areas where you don't have to worry about learning too much from scratch too soon. Specifically, there are numerous different basic strategies that you can use as a way of focusing on the types of skills you are learning in a productive direction. When it comes to planning out your ultimate rates of success, it is important to keep in mind that while the following strategies are certainly going to help you to improve your overall success rate, it is still never going to be a sure thing. No matter how good at trading options you are, losing out on a trade that appeared to be a sure thing is always going to be a part of the process.

The buy-write: This strategy is also known as a covered call and it is ideal if you are unsure about a specific underlying stock because it lets you buy in with confidence regardless of the current market conditions. How it works is that after you purchase the underlying stock in question, you go ahead and create a call that is set to the number of the underlying shares of stock that you now own. This is a great option if you are going to be otherwise occupied in the near future and don't want to worry about the underlying stock as you know that you will still be seeing the benefits of premiums if nothing else. It will also help you to protect investments that were made on a longer time frame as you will know that you will be able to hold onto a profitable sale price if nothing else. This strategy can be especially useful when paired with LEAPS, funds that were purchased via a margin and index futures as well as traditional stocks.

Bull call spread: To use this strategy, you will want to start by purchasing a call option at a strike price you believe to be beneficial. You will then want to sell a similar number of calls at a higher strike price. Both calls should have the same underlying asset and the same timeframe. This is a useful strategy to use if you are bullish on the strength of the underlying asset in question and your research indicates that the price is likely to increase in the time frame you have chosen.

This strategy is also known as a vertical credit spread because it has a pair of mismatched legs. Legs that are sold close to the money generate a credit spread that typically contains a net credit along with a positive time value. On the other hand, a debit spread is created with a short option that ends further from the money than when it started. Overall, this strategy is considered a net buy.

Bear put spread: The bear put spread is similar to the bull call spread but is used in opposite circumstances. Specifically, you begin by purchasing a pair of put options, one at a higher strike price and another at a lower strike price. You are going to want to purchase an equal number of each and ensure that they have the same underlying asset and timeframe. This strategy is useful when you feel bearish on the underlying asset in question as it helps you limit your losses if you are incorrect about the way the market is moving.

The ideal time to use a bear put spread is if you are interested in short selling an underlying asset and using a more common put option doesn't seem to be the right choice. You will find them useful if you are interested in speculating that prices are on a downward trend and don't want to invest a larger amount of capital waiting for the worst to happen. When using a bear put spread you are literally planning for the worst while hoping for the best.

Long combination: Also known as the synthetic long stock strategy, the long combination is utilized by purchasing a call and a put with the same details at the same strike price. You will want the underlying asset price to be quite close to the strike price when you pull the trigger. This is a bullish strategy and the short put is uncovered which leaves you with a significant amount of risk if things go wrong. As such, this strategy is only recommended when the indicators you favor show that the market is likely to move in the way you expect.

This strategy is known as the synthetic long stock due to the fact that the risk and reward are nearly the same as the more common long stock strategy. Additionally, if you hold onto the position until it expires you will likely end up purchasing the underlying asset anyway. Specifically, if the underlying asset ends up higher than the strike price then you will want to exercise the call. Meanwhile, if it is below the strike price it is very likely that the put will be assigned which means you will still need to purchase the asset.

With that being said, there is no limit to how much you want the underlying asset to move once you have set up this strategy, the more positive momentum it has the more money you stand to make. The maximum amount you can expect to lose if things don't go according to plan is limited to the amount of the strike price plus the net debit or minus the net credit.

In this case, purchasing the call will give you the right to purchase the underlying asset at the strike price. Selling the put at the same price then obligates you to purchase the underlying asset at this price if you find yourself in a situation where the option is assigned.

Time decay is a relatively neutral factor for this strategy. On one hand, it will erode the value of the purchased option which is far from ideal. On the other hand, it will also decrease the value of the option being sold.

Butterfly spread: The basic butterfly spread can be performed by simply entering puts or calls at a rate of 1/2/1. Essentially, the trader will buy a single call at one strike price, sell 2 calls that garner a greater strike price and then an additional single call at a price above either of the other two. If the trader is instead utilizing puts the trader will instead buy a single put at a strike price, sell 2 more puts at a low strike price and then buys a final put at a strike price that is lower still. Ideally, the strike price of the option that the trader choses to sell will be at roughly the price the related security is currently worth while the other 2 will be above and below respectively.

If everything goes according to plan, this scenario will then result in a neutral trade that will guarantee that the trader will see a positive return as long as the security in question stays in the anticipated price range. This method can also be used to make directional trades by setting two of the strike prices above the current price of the related security. When done correctly, the butterfly spread creates a fairly low and clearly defined risk that also has a solid chance of potential profit and a high likelihood of a significant return rate.

The modified butterfly spread method differs from the standard butterfly spread in several important ways. First, it allows puts to be used to ensure trades that are bullish and calls to be used to create trades that are bearish. This is thanks in large part to the extended ratio of 1/3/2 and the fact that it has only a single price point that can be considered breakeven which creates a cushion that provides the trader additional leeway.

For example, say that an underlying asset is currently being sold for $194 per share. To activate the modified butterfly, you are going to want to activate the first put at $193.50, three more at $190 and then the final pair at $175. The key takeaway from this example is that puts are selling at 5 points beneath the at the money point and another at 20 points below. As the price is currently at $194 this means that you will be able to breakeven if the price drops to $184 which means that the strategy generates 5 percent worth of downside protection.

This means that the underlying asset in question would need to drop a total of more than 5 percent before any type of loss would occur. In this example, the total potential loss is approximately $2,000 which equals the amount required to put the trade into action. In this case, the loss would not occur until the underlying asset dropped to a price that is lower than $175. On the other hand, the amount you stand to gain from the aforementioned trade equates to about $1,000 which is a 50 percent return on your investment assuming the underlying asset only increases to $200. The strategy would also result in a $500 profit as long as the underlying asset doesn't move past $195.

While the modified variation of the butterfly spread contains a greater degree of risk than the standard version, it also offers a higher profit to risk ratio. It is most useful when you believe the underlying asset is likely to remain stable over the timeframe you have chosen or when you are looking to profit from capital gains on an underlying asset that is likely to remain in the middle of the road.

Vertical spread: A vertical spread is a variation of the common spread option where the pair of options that you purchased, one long and one short, have different strike prices and the same date of expiration. For example, if you purchase a stock's option for $60 while simultaneously selling it for $70 then you will have created a vertical spread.

To fully understand this strategy, assume that you own the underlying stock to a specific option and the stock is currently worth $50, though you anticipate it rising to at least $55 relatively quickly. To take advantage of this fact, you would want to execute a vertical spread. This means you would purchase a call for $50 and simultaneously sell a put for $55. The $50 call is already going to be in the money so it will have a premium of $1. The $55 put will have a 25-cent premium as it is currently out of the money. This means you would pay the $1 and make the 25 cents leaving you with a cost of 75 cents to orchestrate it.

With your setup in place, there are one 2 possible results. The stock will increase in price as you were anticipating or it will drop unexpectedly. If you end up making a poor prediction and watch the price drop to $45 from $50 then both calls will expire out of the money and you will just be out 75 cents. However, if the price rises as you have reason to believe it will, then the price is now $55 which means both your options have premiums, the first of $6 and the second of $1. The call you sold then becomes a naked call and you will need to close out your position prior to the expiration date of the options to protect yourself.

You would then need to sell the $50 call for a profit while also buying back the $55 call that was previously sold. You would then be able to sell the call for $6 and, after that, purchase the other for $1.

Bollinger Bands: Bollinger Bands can be used to trade options successfully because they are an effective signal when it comes to markets being overbought or oversold as options strategies tend to work best when assets are in one of these extremes as part of a trend.

The default Bollinger band setting is based on the 20-day moving average and has two standard deviations. The upper band is typically 2 standard deviations above the 20-day moving average and the lower band is set 2 standard deviations below the 20-day moving average. The underlying asset then trades between these two prices with oversold levels reaching the lower band and overbought levels toughing the upper band. The band's width then represents the volatility of the underlying asset.

In general, assuming that the market is in an uptrend, you will want to use the overbought readings of the Bollinger band to purchase calls or sell puts depending on the strength of your convictions that the trend will continue as well as your overall aversion to risk. If the price hits the higher of the two bands then you will want to take some profits from the expectation of a revision of mean or through the digestion of the overbought conditions.

If you are a more aggressive trader then you may even want to consider buying puts or selling calls. If the market is currently in a downtrend then the choices you make would be reversed.

Bollinger band strategies tend to be the most effective in markets that are currently trendless. Under these market conditions, oversold and overbought readings are always going to be more potent. This is due to the fact that competing forces are currently pulling the market in both directions.

It is also important to keep in mind that price has a strong preference towards fluctuation when it comes to the central band. You will need to be able to detect this fact reliably if you want to successfully make use of any of the strategies outlined below. You will also need to be aware that the top band acts as resistance while the bottom one acts as support.

Covered call: The premise of this strategy is to hold an asset, while writing calls on the same asset in the short term. You will collect the premiums on the contracts that you do write and will know your total level of exposure based on having all of the values for how much you purchased the underlying asset, how much you sold each contract for, and how many contracts you have in circulation.

The first step in this strategy is to purchase an asset. You decide to buy company X; it is currently trading at $3.50 per share. You purchase a total number of shares equal to the number of contracts that you plan on writing. For this example you will be writing just one contract, so you will be buying 100 shares of company X. This costs you a total of $350; as you can see the amount of investment capital you start with greatly limits or enhances your ability to work with these strategies.

After buying the 100 shares, you write a call option with an expiration date of one month from now. The strike price of the option and exercise price will simply be the average of the market index. What you are hoping for is that this stock has very little movement and never reaches the exercise price. Let's say that you sell this option for $150. This puts your total risk at $200. This is calculated by the $350 you spent on the stock and then the $150 you gained from selling an option on this asset. There are three different ways that this investment can go.

First, the exercise price is never met and at the end of the month, the stock price has had very little movement. Second, the exercise price is never met but the price of the stock falls significantly. Finally, the exercise price is met and you have to supply 100 shares of company X to the buyer of the call you sold. This is the worst case scenario for you. You lose the 100 shares of company X but you keep the premium on the call that you sold.

Hedging: When you hedge an option, what you're essentially doing is providing yourself with security in other investments that are already in your portfolio. For example, let's say that you own some stocks. They're high priced, and you really have no idea of knowing whether or not they're going to appreciate over the long-term; however, you know that you want to stick with this stock for the long-term because this is part of your long-term investment strategy.

Instead of simply hoping for the best even though you know that company in which you've invested is going through a rough patch, you are looking for more security. You decide that you're going to invest in an option, but in a way that counteracts the decisions that you've made regarding the activity that you've already invested in with the long-term stocks that you already own.

Some common examples of hedging include taking out insurance that will minimize your income's exposure to risk in the unfortunate event of your death and paying the money back in monthly sums rather than in one huge payment over a period of time. While these are great examples of hedging because you are able to see how leveraging is working on a smaller scale, the big stock market players see hedging a bit differently. To conglomerates such as the New York Stock Exchange, hedging is a bit different in the sense that it is typically used in a way that will counter the potential for competitors within an industry to cause you to lose money.

One of the biggest reasons why using options as a way to hedge is because of the ability for the hedge to transfer and diminish risk. Not only can hedging help to alleviate the stress that risk plays on your portfolio as a whole, but it can also serve to pacify other stressors of life as well.

Chapter 5: Mistakes to Avoid

Not focusing on discipline: Many new traders find themselves going after specific options or types of options simply because they have a gut feeling. Unfortunately, very few people can effectively trust their gut when it comes to trading options which means this scattershot policy will not only make it more difficult for you make a profit overall, but it can teach you bad habits along the way as well. As such, rather than focusing on what your gut is telling you, a better choice is to instead work on building your trading discipline by following the rules outlined below with every single trade you make. It might be hard to go against your gut at first, but over time you will be glad you did.

It doesn't matter if you feel that a specific price for a given option is too high or too low, the only thing you can reliably focus on at the moment is the price as it currently stands. If the facts say that an option should be valued higher, you buy, if it says lower you sell, end of story. It is important to remain impartial about every stock you purchase as forming an attachment is the surest way to lose objectivity.

Once you have formed a successful plan, following it to the letter every time is always going to be the logical choice. As such, if you follow your plan to the letter and a trade doesn't work out in the way that you expect there is no reason angry with yourself as you still made the proper choice. As long as your plan returns positive results more than 50 percent of the time you are going to make a profit, keep this in mind and you will see the failed trades for what they are, the statistical balance to the rest of your success.

Not trading mechanically: As a new options trader, it can seem like the easiest way to improve may be to spend more time looking for ways to predict the ways the market is going to move. Unfortunately, predicting the market the way most people think of it is rarely possible, as there are simply too many variables to successfully chart them all. Fortunately, you don't need to be able to predict the market in order to be successful, all you really need to do is follow existing trends.

When it comes to following existing trends, often the easiest way to do this is to have a solid plan ahead of time and them follow that plan religiously. This will likely be harder than it first appears, however, as there will be emotions and ego vying for your time and actions. It is important to work to ignore losses as long as they are within predetermined levels of acceptability. Collectively this is referred to as acting mechanically and your goal should ultimately be to act completely mechanically in every trade.

Reaching the 100 percent mechanical trading state means you never actually have to make any decisions; the entire process simply follows the plan. Your goal should then to ultimately never have to monitor the activity of the market and follow through on the actions the plan dictates. If instead you find yourself making most of your trades on a whim and listening to your gut more than whatever system or plan you have, then you are a judgmental trader and will likely find it difficult to learn from your mistakes. This is because not every correct decision leads to gains nor does every poor decision lead to losses, without these types of constants flying by the seat of your pants will always ultimately lead to disaster.

It is human nature to build stories around, and therefore form relationships with, all manner of inanimate objects including individual options This is why it is perfectly natural to feel a closer connection to particular trades, and possibly even consider throwing out your plan when one of them takes an unexpected dive. Thinking about and acting on are two very different things, however, which is why being aware of these tendencies is so important in avoiding them at all costs.

This scenario happens just as frequently with trades moving in positive directions as it does negative, but the results are always going to be the same. Specifically, it can be extremely tempting to hang on to a given trade much longer than you might otherwise decide to simply because it is on a hot streak that shows no sign of stopping but it is still the wrong move in the long-term.

Not understanding market forces: While you will likely run into countless different scenarios that cause stock prices to rise and fall during your time working with the stock market, the fact of the matter is that every day the majority of all of the market movement that you encounter is going to be traced quite directly back to the interchange between supply and demand. If a company has good news to report then the demand for that stock is going to increase, much like the supply of available stock would become greater if the company reported the negative news instead. While this idea is simple, the ways it plays out can easily become quite complex.

While things can be relatively straightforward if the news is clearly good or bad, determining which is which can often be more difficult than that which is why it is important to do your research on companies you are interested in beforehand to ensure that when news breaks, you understand what it means. While doing research, it is important to keep in mind that the current value of the stock can easily be different than what the company is currently worth, instead, you need to factor the current price of the stock versus the total number of shares that are currently in play. As such, if you have a company with a stock that is worth just $5, but they currently have 5 million shares in the wild then that company is still worth 25 million dollars.

When you are researching various companies, you are also going to want to keep in mind the fact that they are generally evaluated based on investor expectations regarding their future earnings. When it comes to looking at earnings, what you are really seeing is the sum total of what the company has made in the past 3 months with all of the costs taken out.

Never let your losses build: As a new trader, it can be easy to become emotionally invested in the options you choose which is why it is crucial that you learn to separate your expectations for a trade from the reality of what occurs when the rubber meets the road. To successfully ensure that you don't lose more than the bare minimum on a given trade it is important that you cut it lose the second it stops generating a profit as opposed to hanging on to it in hopes that it turns around and rebounds in the correct direction.

It is important to learn early that a failed trade is not a reflection on you as a trader but simply a part of the natural trading process. Sticking with a losing trade is rarely, if ever, going to result in that trade turning around, and if it does the results are going to be middling at best. Likewise, it is never a good idea to double down on a losing trade as a means of mitigating a potential loss. Adding to a losing position is akin to trying to dig yourself out of a hole, it is never going to work no matter how hard you want it to.

Not keeping a trading journal : While it might seem to be a waste of time at first, the fact of the matter is that keeping a journal of all of the trades you make can be an extremely effective way to analyze what you are doing right, as well as what you are doing wrong when it comes to options trading. While one type of analysis or the other might peak your interest when it comes to trading at the moment, keeping a trading journal will allow you to look at your trading results from a more analytical perspective once you have gotten a little more distance and perspective on what it is that you are doing.

To get the most out of this process you are going to want to keep track of each trade you make along with the date, the state of the market and the underlying asset that you were basing all of your trades on, whether the trade ended up being profitable or not and your emotional and mental state while you were trading. While trying to find patterns in your trading style every day, or even every week, won't necessarily provide you with the information you are looking for, looking back on what you have accomplished about once a month with provide you with enough data to actually make informed decisions and will help you track your progress as well whether or not any changes end up needing to be made.

Following relative trends : Existing trends in the market can be a potential signpost for future movement but they are far from guaranteed. It is completely natural for the market to fluctuate as much as 20 percent on either side of the average at any given time. As such, if you jump on an apparent trend without researching it thoroughly you can find yourself attached to a momentum play that will never materialize. Instead, it is important to consider each apparent trend through the lens of three distinct time frames for the best results. If you are fond of short-term trades then daily, hourly and weekly charts are recommended. If you prefer long-term trades then you will want to stick to weekly, daily and monthly charts instead.

Not getting while the getting is good: Many traders have an adequate entry plan but then move forward without determining an exit plan that is just as effective. This, in turn, leads to scenarios where they either get out too early, too late or end up with an investment instead of a trade. If you find it difficult to know when to exit gracefully, you will want to focus on adding detailed technical specifications to your exit strategy. Once you put these specifics into place, it is important to monitor them and change them as needed as the market evolves. While early on it is sure to feel as though the profits you see are the only profits you are ever going to see, you need to work to avoid this impulse. Giving in to it is sure to cause you to lose out on far more profits than it would ever generate.

Wasting time trying to get even : If you ever hope to be a master trader then you need to factor failure into your long-term plan. Not only will this make it easier to prevent emotion from getting the better of you, but it will also help you make fewer mistakes down the line as well. Remember, it is important to focus exclusively on the numbers and not pin your self-esteem or personal image to individual trades. Focusing on the price action will allow you to block out thoughts about breaking even or magic numbers and improve your trade percentage as a result. Determining if a day was a success or a failure isn't something you can do until the market closes and it is useless, and destructive, to try.

Not being upfront about your flaws: The best traders aren't the ones that never make mistakes and are all around perfect in every way; rather, they are the ones who are completely comfortable with their weaknesses and understand how to use their strengths in such a way that everything balances out. As such, if you are looking to improve your overall trading performance then a good place to start is accepting your weaknesses instead of pretending they are not there. Shoring up these weak points will go a long way towards helping you reach the financial success that you are looking for.

Not being decisive: If you hope to ever be considered an expert trader then you are going to need to understand not just how to do the research and then use it to pinpoint good points of entrance and exit, you are going to need to know when to go ahead and jump in with both feet even if you aren't 100 percent sure that the trade is going to end in success. The fact of the matter is that it doesn't matter how good you are at finding potentially profitable trades, all that matters is your ability to close trades successfully, everything else is just a means to an end.

This doesn't mean you need to be lucky or listen to your gut, it means you need to be able to accurately read a specific situation in real time and then process all the disparate data quickly enough to make a relevant decision before time runs out. While it might seem impossible at first, it will get easier with time.

Not keeping your mindset in mind : If you ever want to hope to truly make money successfully trading then there are several skills that you are going to need to hone to a fine point to ensure that your trading game is on point. The most important of these is ensuring that you develop the right mindset to trade successfully and, more importantly, that you automatically start to utilize it without thinking about it. Specifically, you are going to want to make a concentrated effort to always keep a cool head, regardless of how good, or bad, the current situation might appear. When trading, your ultimate goal should be to remain as emotionless as possible and to not let any thoughts not related to trading based on your plan enter into the equation at all.

While it likely seems fairly obvious that emotions don't have a place in your trading plan, understanding this fact and acting to ensure that you trade with robotic precision are two separate things. While banishing all emotions at once, especially if you are naturally an emotional person, can be tricky, the best way to go about doing it successfully is by working to remove the influence of one emotion at a time.

The first emotion that you are going to need to deal with is anger as it can easily cloud your judgment with you even realizing it. It is natural to feel angry when a trade that is going your way suddenly turns around and starts moving in the other direction, however, that doesn't mean that acting on the anger is going to do you any good in the long run. Instead of letting your anger influence your decision-making process, you need to get into the habit of working quickly to minimize your losses and leaving the feelings of anger to cool on the backburner until you have alleviated the situation as much as possible.

Conclusion

Thanks for making it through to the end of *Options Trading For Beginners: How To Start*, let's hope it was informative and able to provide you with all of the tools you need to achieve your goals, whatever it is that they may be. Just because you've finished this book doesn't mean there is nothing left to learn on the topic, and expanding your horizons is the only way to find the mastery you seek.

Now that you have made it to the end of this book, you hopefully have an understanding of how to get started in the world of options trading, as well as a strategy or two, or three, that you are anxious to try. Before you go ahead and put your money where your mouth is, however, it is important that you have realistic expectations as to the level of success you should expect in the near future.

While it is perfectly true that some people experience serious success right out of the gate when trading options, it is an unfortunate fact that they are the exception rather than the rule. What this means is that you should expect to experience something of a learning curve, especially when you are first getting your new trading plan up and running. Instead, you should think of your time spent trading options as a marathon rather than a sprint which means that slow and steady will win the race every single time.

Finally, if you found this book useful in anyway, a review on Amazon is always appreciated!

Description

While the steep barrier to entry surrounding the stock market means that it is out of reach for many people, options trading offers an affordable alternative that still promises the opportunity for plenty of profit. If you are interested in learning how to stop living paycheck to paycheck and how to start putting your money to work for you then *Option Trading For Beginners: How To Start* is the book you have been waiting for.

Inside you will find everything you need to know to dip your toe in options trading without ending up all wet. First, you will learn about what sets options trading apart from securities trading. Next, you will learn to create a trading plan that will prevent you from losing your shirt. From there you will learn about the technical indicators to watch when it comes to picking potential trades as well as plenty of starter strategies to try. Finally, you will find an assortment of common mistakes that new options traders make as well as steps you can take to ensure you do not follow in their footsteps.

So, what are you waiting for? Take control of your financial future and buy this book today!

www.ingramcontent.com/pod-product-compliance
Lightning Source LLC
Chambersburg PA
CBHW031558210526
45464CB00003B/1334